This Things That Go sticker
activity book belongs to:

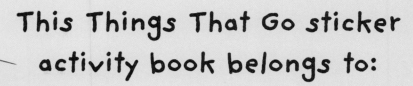

. . . .

These vehicles won't go anywhere without wheels! See if you can find some wheel stickers to add.

bicycle

truck

car

tractor

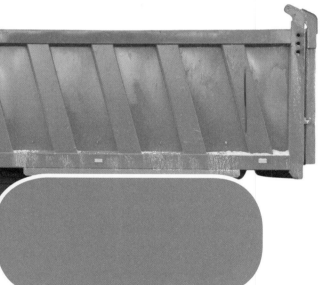

horse and cart

Put some speedy race cars on the track.

Color in this busy ocean scene.

How many boats can you see? How many submarines can you see?

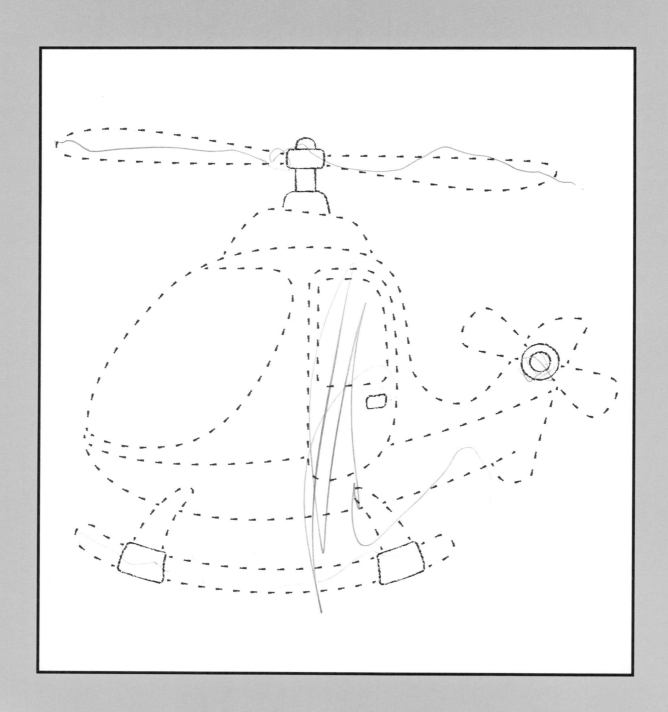

Can you color these in?

Find the missing stickers, then draw a line from the vehicles to the things they carry.

garbage truck

forklift

loader

school bus

rocks

heavy
boxes

children

garbage bags

What's this little car towing?

Now use your imagination to draw what this car is towing.

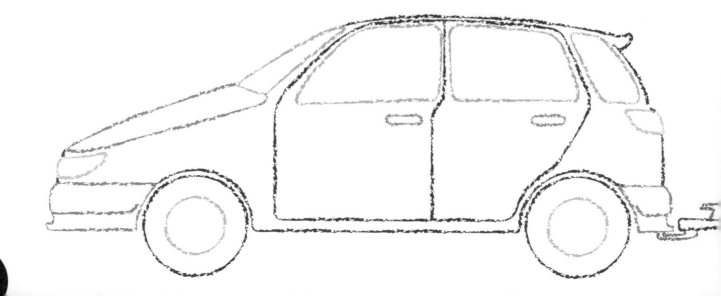

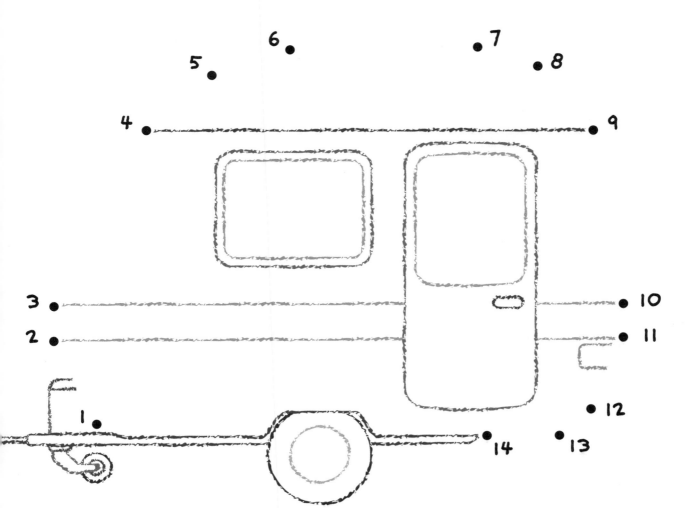

Which train is going to the station?

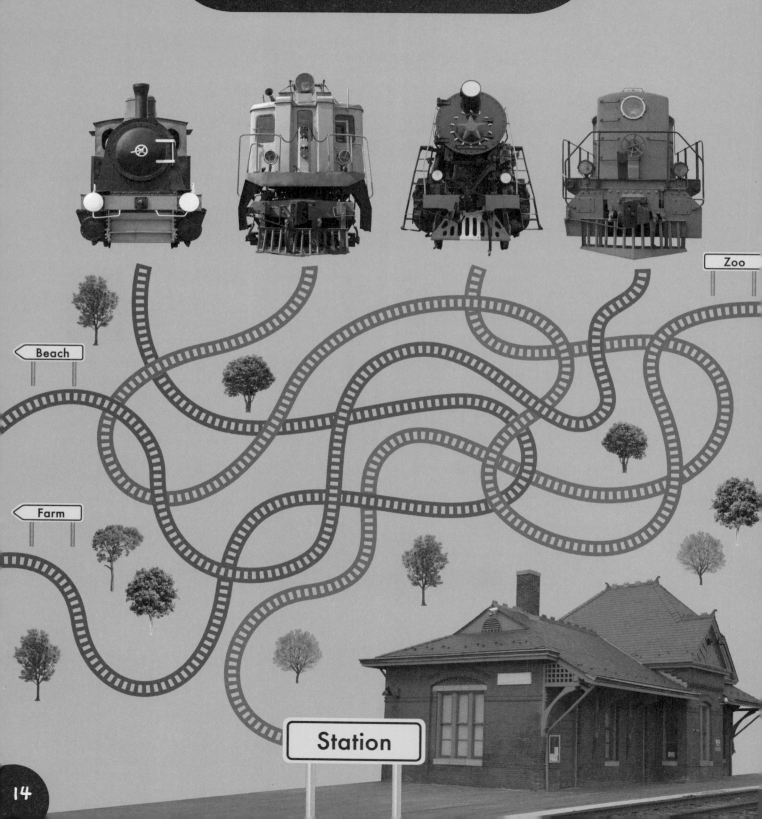

Color in this train and decorate it with stickers.

Add some sailboat stickers to the lake.

Design your own road signs!

Look on the sticker pages
and find the stickers for
these things that go.

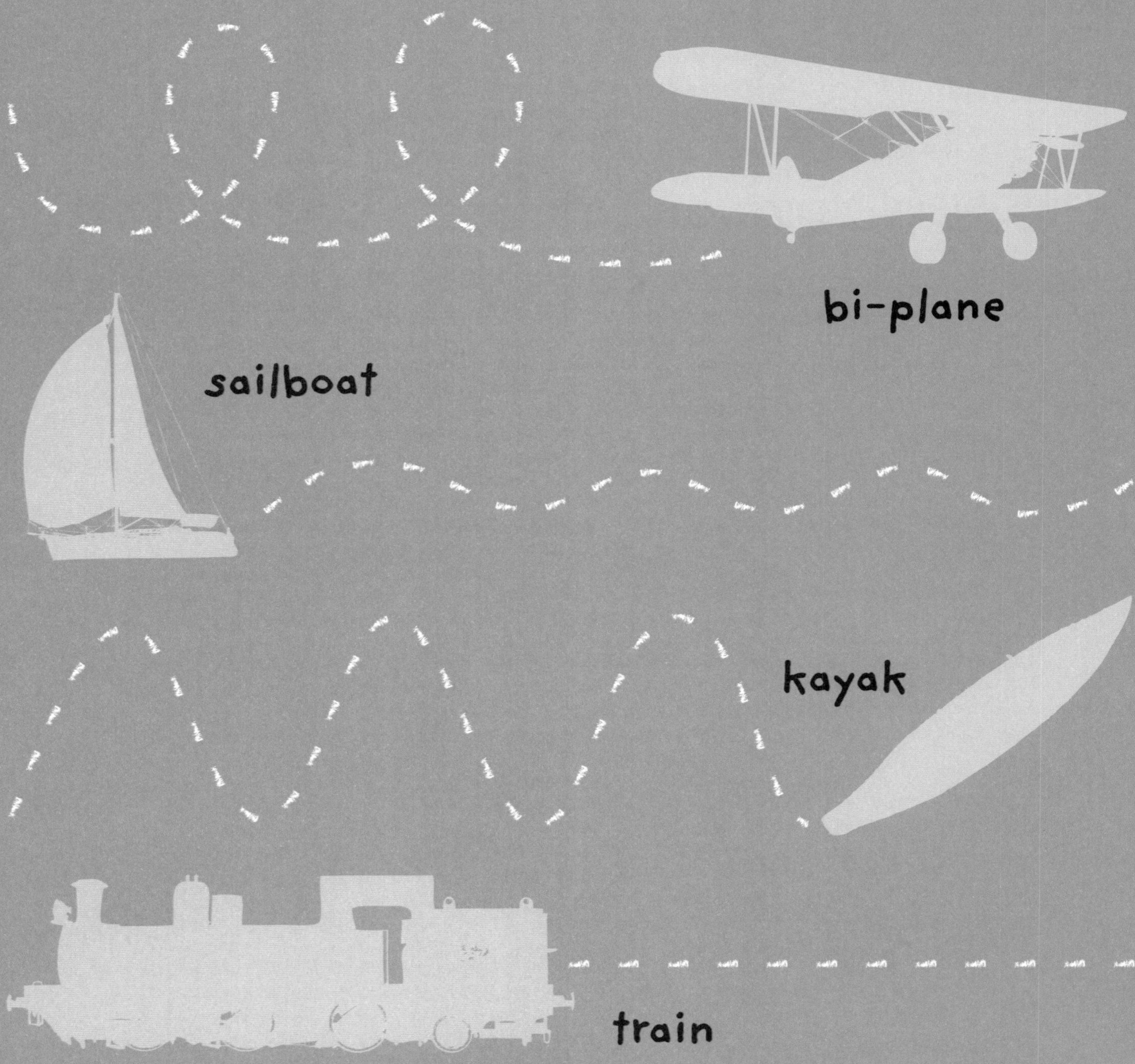

bi-plane

sailboat

kayak

train

Draw a space shuttle for this astronaut.

Monster trucks
can crush cars!
Color this one in
and decorate it.

Now design your own
mighty machine.

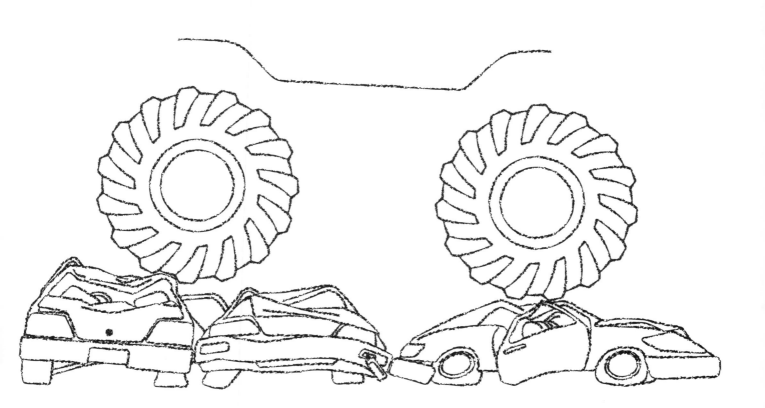

This airport is looking empty! Add some planes and baggage trucks.

Help the police car find the robbers!

Draw your own
police car.

Add a space
shuttle sticker to
zoom to the moon.

Now add some astronaut and
satellite stickers.

Fill the sky with hot air balloon stickers.

How many blue balloons can you count? How many red ones?

Connect the dots to see what's about to blast off.

Can you find 5 differences between these airplanes? Now color them in.

33

Before there were cars, people traveled by horse and buggy. Place the horse and buggy stickers in front of the museum.

Help the truck pick up all the bags and bring them to the recycling center.

recycling center

Use crayons to color
these race cars.

Can you find a snowmobile to zoom down the mountain?

Hang some trams
onto the cables.

Add some airplanes to the sky.

What doesn't belong in the sea in this picture? What doesn't belong in the sky?

Use the grid to copy the sailboat.

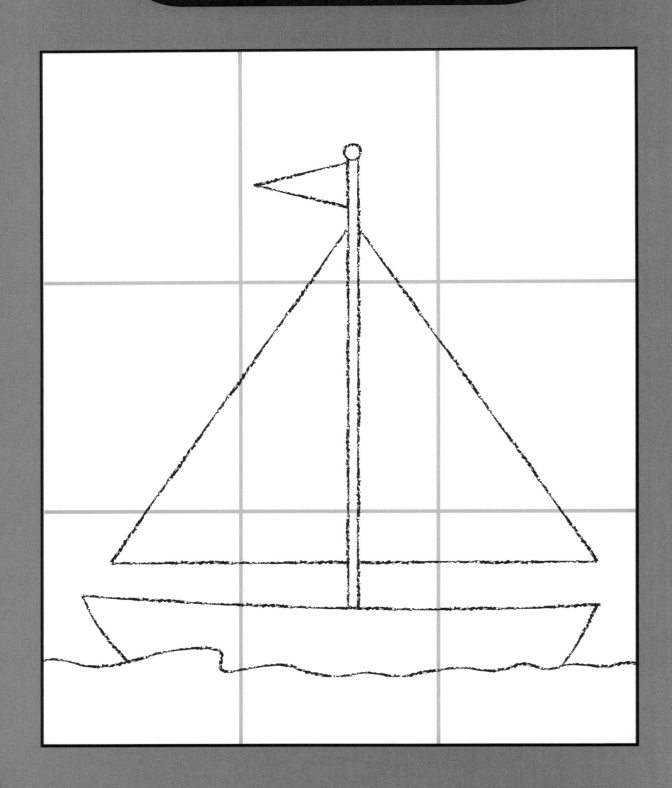

Now color it in.

What a lot of shiny tractors! Find the matching pairs and draw lines to connect them.

What things can you add to the land, water, and sky from the sticker pages?

Bumper cars are designed to crash into each other! Color in these crashing, smashing amusement park rides.

Some bridges open up to let tall boats pass through.

Use your stickers to add some boats to the river and some vehicles to the road.

Find the two trucks that are the same and circle them.

Can you find 5 differences in these pictures?

Helicopters land on helipads. Look for the "H" to see where to put the helicopter sticker.

Use your crayons and your imagination to turn these shapes into vehicles!

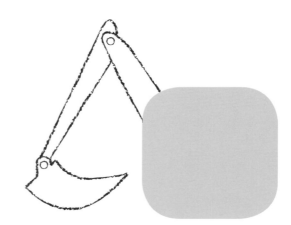

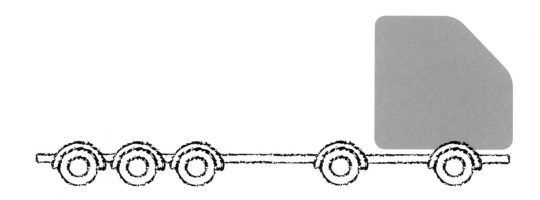

What a busy train station!
Color in the scene.

Add some construction stickers to this scene.

Can you find some boats to float on the water?

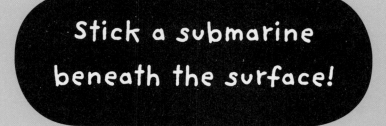

Stick a submarine beneath the surface!

Color in these things that go.

Which one do you
like best, and why?

These huskies are trained to pull sleds. Find the sled sticker to add to the end of the reins.

A monorail is a train that runs on a single track high above the ground.

Can you add a train to the tracks on the ground and to the tunnel below?

Add some cars to this parking garage.

3

2

1

ANSWERS

Pages 6-7: There are 6 boats and 2 submarines.

Pages 10-11:

Pages 12-13: It's a camper!

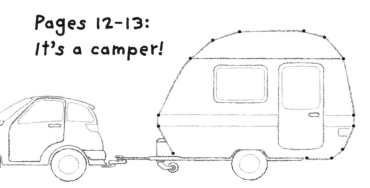

Page 14:

Page 20

train · sailboat · kayak · bi-plane

Page 26:

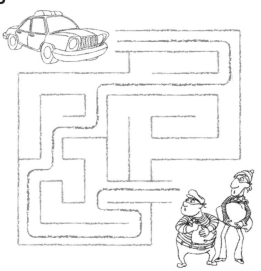

Pages 30-31: There are 3 blue balloons and 5 red balloons.

Page 32:

It's a space shuttle!

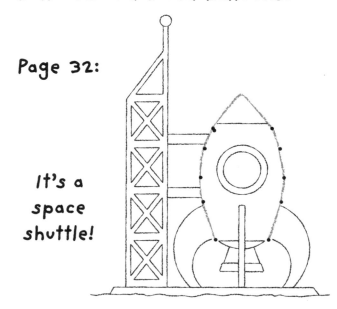

ANSWERS

Page 33:

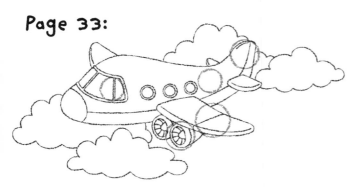

Page 40:

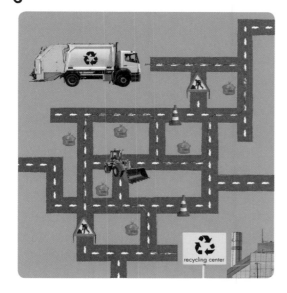

Pages 46-47: The ferry does not belong in the sky. The space shuttle does not belong in the sea.

Pages 50-51:

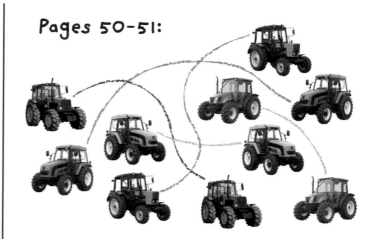

Page 58:

Page 59:

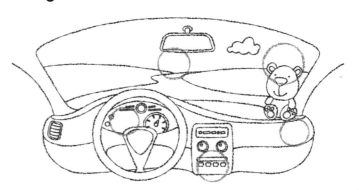

Good-bye, things that go!

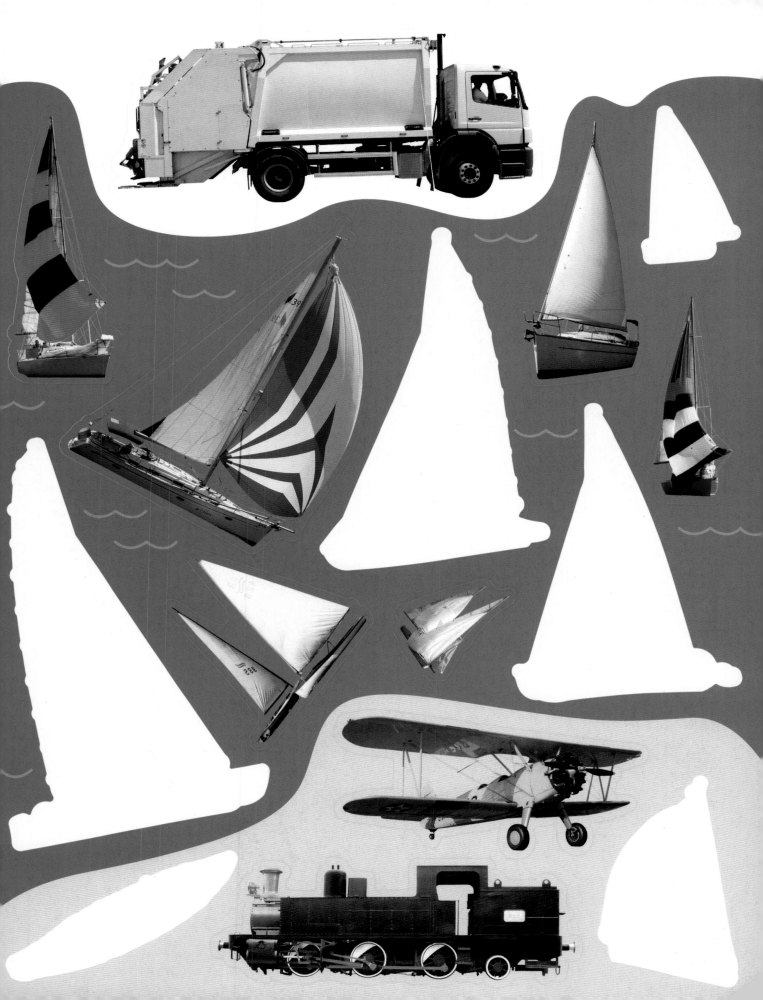

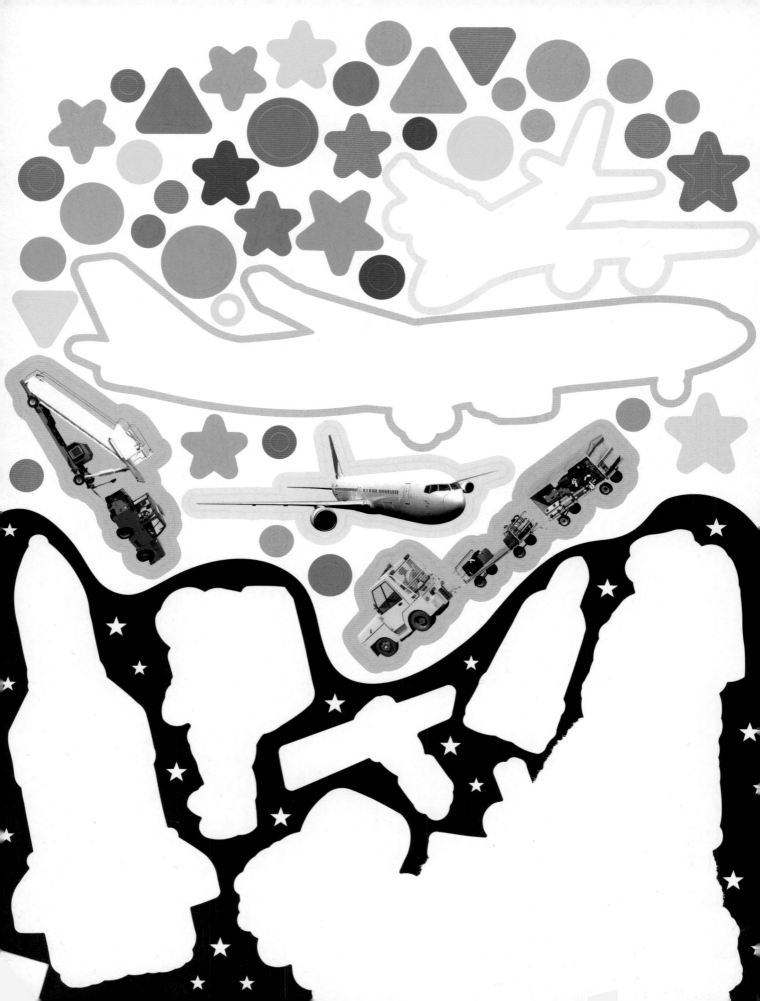

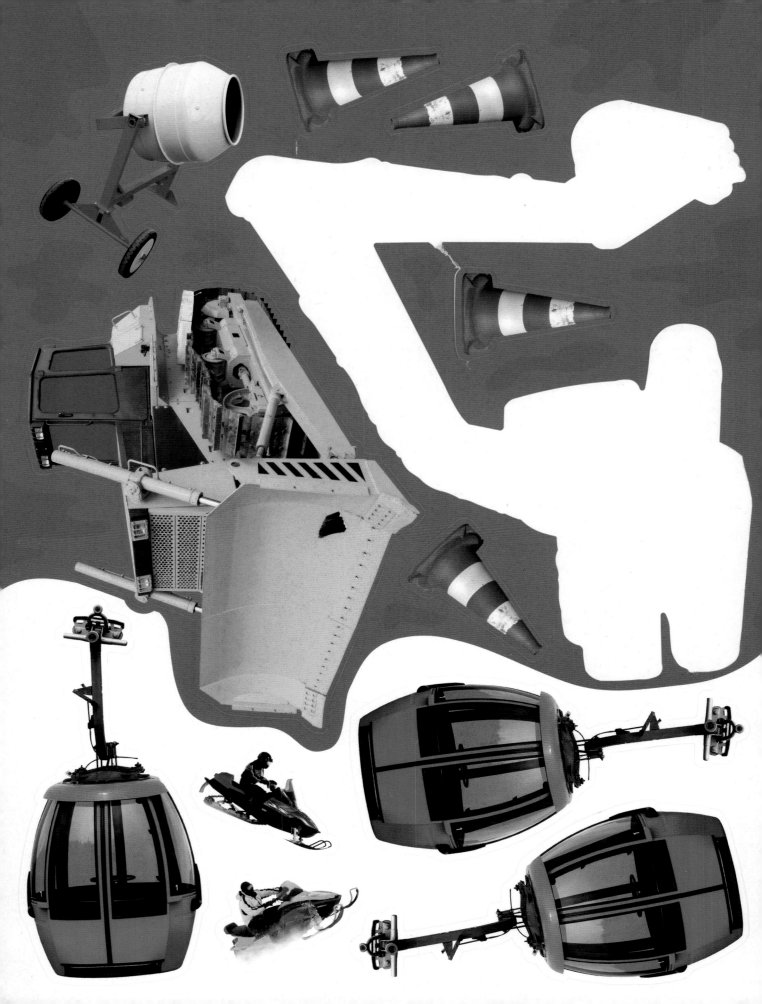